CHANNEL ISLANDS NATIONAL PARK
AND NATIONAL MARINE SANCTUARY

California's Galapagos

CHANNEL ISLANDS NATIONAL PARK
AND NATIONAL MARINE SANCTUARY

California's Galapagos

TIM HAUF

TEXT BY CATHERINE FRENCH

WITH A FOREWORD BY JEAN-MICHEL COUSTEAU

Channel Islands National Park and National Marine Sanctuary: *California's Galapagos*

Photography: All photos © Tim Hauf, except where noted.
Text: Catherine French

Published by Tim Hauf Photography, P.O. Box 1241, Kingston, WA 98346, USA.

Library of Congress Control Number: 2013903382

ISBN: Hardcover – 978-0-9788219-6-8
Soft cover – 978-0-9788219-5-1

Website: *www.timhaufphotography.com*

Email: *timhauf@hotmail.com*

Edited by: Sharon Vincent

Printed and bound in Hong Kong, China

FSC certified paper and eco-friendly inks

Printed on FSC certified (Forest Stewardship Counsel) recycled paper.

Publishing a book of this type requires the involvement of many dedicated and enthusiastic people and organizations to obtain the photos, properly identify the subjects, and verify the accuracy of the information presented.

Tim Hauf wishes to sincerely thank the following for their generous support: Channel Islands National Park, *www.nps.gov/chis*; Channel Islands National Marine Sanctuary, *www.channelislands.noaa.gov*; Island Packers Cruises, *www.islandpackers*.com; NASA/GSFC/LaRC/JPL, MISR Team, for use of the satellite image on the following page; and Richard Salas, *www.askphotography.com*, for his incredible underwater photos which are used in this book.

A special note of appreciation to Jean-Michel Cousteau, *www.oceanfutures.org*.

First printing: September 2013

Page 1: **Inspiration Point, Anacapa Island.**
Page 2-3: **Sunrise, Santa Barbara Island.**
Page 6-7: **Midden site and Northern elephant seals, China Camp beach, Santa Rosa Island.**

SANTA BARBARA

POINT CONCEPTION

VENTURA

LOS ANGELES

SANTA CRUZ ISLAND

SAN MIGUEL ISLAND

ANACAPA ISLAND

SANTA ROSA ISLAND

SANTA CATALINA ISLAND

SANTA BARBARA ISLAND

SAN NICHOLAS ISLAND

SAN CLEMENTE ISLAND

TABLE OF CONTENTS

Snowy plover at Skunk Point, Santa Rosa Island.

FOREWORD
Jean-Michel Cousteau

Since first being thrown overboard by my late father, Jacques-Yves Cousteau at the age of seven with a tank on my back, I have been compelled to explore, to discover, to understand the secrets of the sea. An oft-quoted fact is that we know more about the surface of the moon than we do about our oceans. How can we protect what we don't understand? Ironically, as we have explored and learned more about ecological processes within the oceans and made great discoveries about the vast diversity of life in just the past 50 years, we have also degraded, overfished and changed the basic chemistry of the oceans faster than any time in recorded history. We now know the oceans sustain all life on this planet; but we are threatening the very fabric of what holds our rich tapestry of biodiversity together.

When I first came to Santa Barbara in 1968, I discovered that I could look across the channel and see islands and it reminded me of home in Southern France. I have always been drawn to these Channel Islands; their mere presence overwhelms my senses.

Within Channel Islands National Park and the Channel Islands National Marine Sanctuary, warm southern currents, and cold, nutrient rich northern currents mix around five islands, in the sanctuary so close to a highly populated mainland. The few traffic jams here involve only sea lions. It is truly an American Treasure, for us to all appreciate and protect. I always look forward to every opportunity I get to cross one of the richest bodies of water, the Santa Barbara Channel, and plunge into the depths of the lush giant kelp forests found just offshore of the islands.

Soon after my father passed away in 1997, I had a most memorable moment in the Landing Cove at Anacapa Island, a place that has been a marine protected area since 1980. This was the first time I was back in the water after my father's funeral, and to be able to dive into the depths of a protected area was like exploring uncharted reefs and rocky shorelines with my father and the Cousteau team years ago with abundance, diversity and rich productivity.

The more I learn about the ocean, the more I realize how little I truly understand it. Even after all these years, a sense of exploration and wonder still fills me each time I dive into the oceans' depths. When I visit Channel Islands National Park and the National Marine Sanctuary, I am thankful for these wild places.

The images in this book will transport you on a journey of discovery while allowing you to take a step back in time. You will get a taste of these special places and will hopefully understand the importance of nature's work and our species taking care of the gift we have received from nature for all time.

I know that when people see and feel the beauty of the undersea world and protected isolated islands, they understand in a profound way the need to take care of our water planet and special places like the Channel Islands. Creative, optimistic, inspirational people are the force of a better future. Tim Hauf is that type of person, and through his beautiful images he gives us that sense of personal connection to do all that you can to be a part of a sustainable future. I always say, protect the oceans and you protect yourself. Dive in and enjoy the beauty of Channel Islands National Park and Channel Islands National Marine Sanctuary. They are yours to protect and to love.

CALIFORNIA'S GALAPAGOS
introduction

As the morning mist rises, California's offshore islands begin to appear through the early morning fog. Since the first human stepped foot on these remote isles, the Channel Islands have beckoned us to enjoy their diverse landscapes, to stroll on pristine beaches and to partake of the isolated wilderness. Here we breathe fresh air, walk on undeveloped land as did the people who came before us, and marvel in the natural flora and fauna of these remote ecosystems.

Today, a visit to Channel Islands National Park provides a glimpse into a time before sea travel was available to everyday people and the islands were but a distant dream. Located just miles offshore of the metropolis of Los Angeles, these isolated islands include 13,000 years of Native American history, a rich ranching past spanning over 150 years, and plant and animal species unique to the Channel Islands and found nowhere else on earth.

Of the eight Channel Islands off the California coast, five make up Channel Islands National Park–Anacapa, Santa Cruz, Santa Rosa, San Miguel, and Santa Barbara islands. The islands make up only a part of this special place as the park boundaries extend one nautical mile offshore around each island, making it an "aquatic" park as well.

In 1980, this rare ecosystem became a National Park for 145 rare and endemic species of plants and animals. At the same time, the offshore waters that extend six nautical miles from mean high tide were designated as a National Marine Sanctuary to manage and help protect diverse marine life, habitats, and maritime heritage resources. Since 1976, this unique environment became part of the UNESCO international biosphere preserve program.

Left: **Harbor seals at Southeast Anchorage, Santa Rosa Island.**
Right: **Side-blotched lizard.**

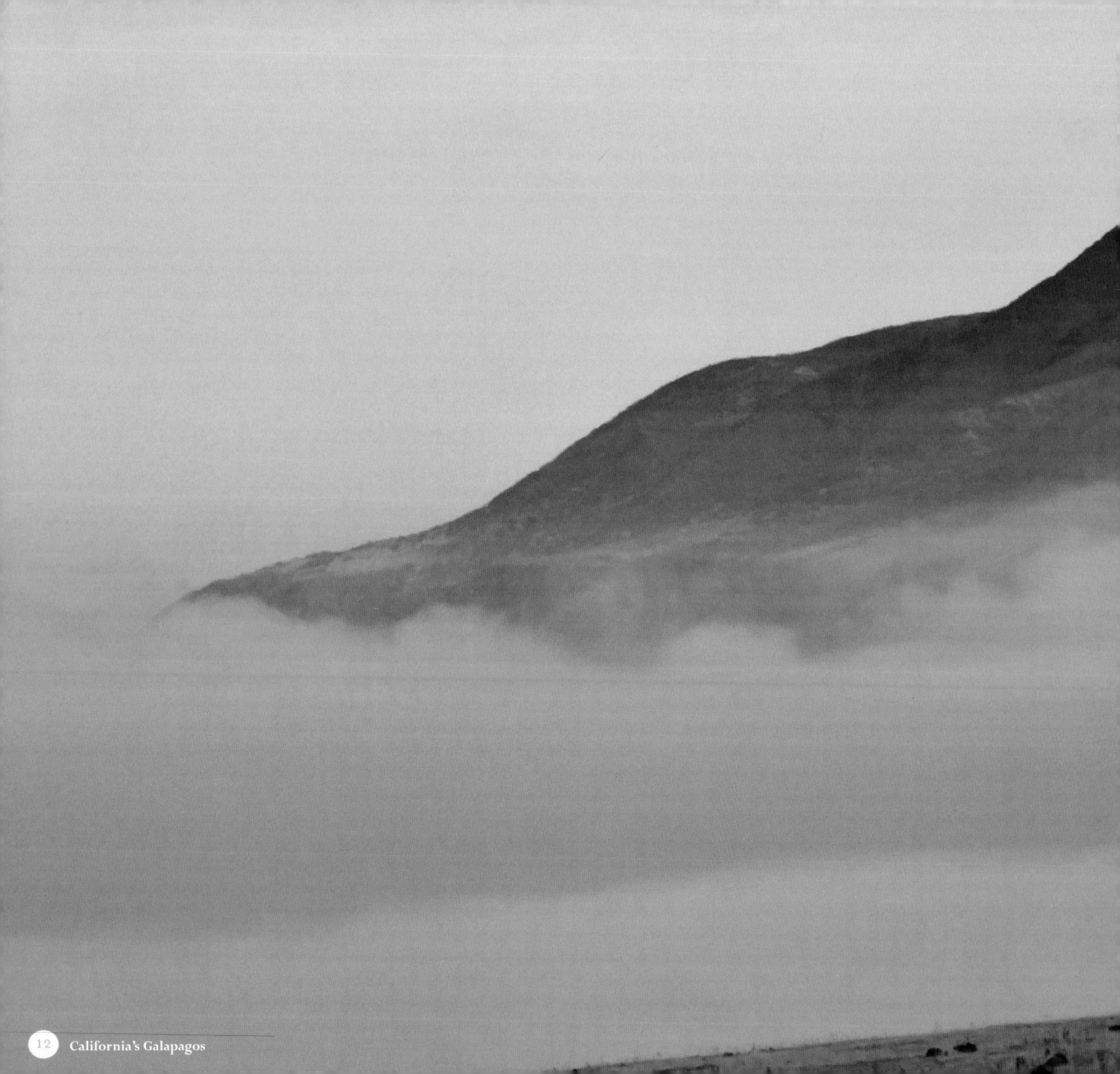

ISLANDS RISING FROM THE SEA

The remote nature of these islands is what makes them unique on our planet. Because these islands have always been separate from the mainland, isolation has played a significant role in the development of the special flora and fauna found here. It is an ancient story dating back over 100 million years.

Until about 30 million years ago, two large tectonic plates of the Earth's crust converged on the western edge of North America. A marine basin formed near the land and for millions of years the sediments that washed off the land into this basin collected and solidified to become some of the sedimentary rocks found on the islands today.

Millions of years later, the Pacific Plate made contact with the North American Plate and continental pieces began to break off and join the Pacific Plate. This slow process eventually created the modern San Andreas boundary. In Southern California, the two plates are sliding by each other, moving laterally in opposite directions along the San Andreas Fault.

Five million years before present time, uplifting of the islands and their east-west orientation were a direct result of the plate tectonic forces. At that time, the four northern Channel Islands made up a super island scientists call *Santarosae*. Because of the current interglacial period or "ice melt," the sea level rising over 18,000 years has separated these four islands. Moreover, this increased sea level reduced the islands and mainland shorelines, furthering their distance apart from each other and the mainland.

Natural plant and animal communities thrived in this isolation for thousands of years making their adaptations unique. In recent times, human activities and the introduction of non-native plants and animals have resulted in the extinction of some endemic flora and fauna and others are now endangered as well.

Through the combined efforts of Channel Islands National Park, The Nature Conservancy, and a network of partners, work is continuing to reestablish and rehabilitate the islands' diverse native plant communities and bird habitats. Other efforts extend offshore to help protect the delicate marine ecosystem and its inhabitants.

The surrounding ocean water is so rich in nutrients that it provides the perfect feeding ground for resident and migrating marine mammals. In fact, over one third of the world's species of whales, dolphins and porpoises live in or come to feed in this region. Seals, sea lions, fish and invertebrates abound in the pristine ocean.

Due to the unique nature of this ecosystem, in 2003 the California Department of Fish and Wildlife established a network of marine protected areas within the park and nearshore waters of the Channel Islands National Marine Sanctuary. In 2007 to add further protection, the National Oceanic and Atmospheric Administration extended these protected zones into deeper waters.

These marine reserves and marine conservation areas encompass 241 square nautical miles (318 square statute miles). However, nearly 80% of the surrounding waters remain open to commercial and recreational anglers who enjoy the bounty of this pristine ocean environment.

The Channel Islands protected areas are in place to help the natural restoration of important habitats and ecosystems while providing a refuge for all sea life and to preserve our nation's natural marine heritage for future generations.

A visit to the park islands provides a glimpse into the California of the 1800s. Each island has its own special allure with diverse native plants and animals as well as stunning panoramic views of the cerulean Pacific Ocean surrounding them.

The islands' story is unique on earth. They are places of natural beauty and bounty that the native Chumash people and their forebears called home for thousands of years. Now, through the lens of award winning photographer Tim Hauf, you too can discover the richness of these remote places and the beauty that lies within Channel Islands National Park.

Above: **Burrowing owl.**
Opposite page: **San Miguel Island fox.**

ANACAPA ISLAND
endless illusion

The native Chumash Indians aptly named the island *Ennepah*—their word for "mirage" or "ever changing"—as it seems to change shape in the summer fog or afternoon heat. Closest to the mainland, three islets make up Anacapa Island. Measuring only one square mile in size and less than 5 miles long, the islets–East, Middle and West–are separated by rocky outcroppings and ocean, making them accessible only by boat.

An abundance of sea birds thrive on this diminutive isle where isolation provides fewer predators and the habitat has not been overly affected by development as on the mainland.

Craggy and steep volcanic cliffs make the islets a perfect home for a variety of birds, like cormorants and the world's largest breeding colony of western gulls that take residence on East Anacapa. Each year, gulls begin their nesting efforts at the end of April with many of their shallow ground nests situated just inches from hiking trails.

Visitors can easily observe the birds on their nests, catch sight of their spotted eggs, and even see hatching chicks between May and June. In July, you can watch mature chicks fly away from their island birthplace.

West Anacapa is home to the largest breeding colony of California brown pelicans, a successfully recovered species that was removed from the endangered list in 2009. Anacapa is also home to one of the rarest sea bird species in the world, the Scripps's murrelet. Once near extinction, this petite night-feeding seabird is recovering following the eradication of non-native black rats in 2002.

Due to the lack of fresh water, the endemic Anacapa deer mouse is the only land mammal on this arid isle. These tiny mice have adapted to this dry environment. Now, without competition from black rats, the population is thriving once again.

A male California brown pelican soars above Inspiration Point.

Island History

In 1932, Anacapa became the site of the last permanent lighthouse built on the west coast of the United States. U.S. Coast Guard personnel manned the lighthouse and lived on Anacapa until 1969, when the light's third order Fresnel lens was decommissioned and an automated beacon installed. Visitors can view this stunning crystal artifact in the island's Visitor Center.

In the 1950s, Coast Guard personnel planted red-flowered ice plant that is native to South Africa for landscaping and erosion control following the building of houses and a road system. The succulent quickly spread around the island, directly affecting other island flora, soon covering most of the landscape. It even affected the native species of giant coreopsis, as it is so efficient at outcompeting the native vegetation. Its quick growth increased the salinity of the soil and covered the ground preventing germination of native seeds.

This small island is home to 265 species of plants, including two that exist only on Anacapa and twenty found only on the Channel Islands. Park staff with the aid of many volunteers and partners are working to restore native plant communities that once thrived on the island.

Arch Rock.

The gradually undulating 1.5 mile hiking trail on East Anacapa provides visitors with stunning island views and dramatic overlooks to the pristine ocean below the plunging cliffs. California sea lions can be heard barking from the rocky beaches below and can be observed feeding in the giant kelp forests in the clear waters.

The sea lions along with harbor seals–part of a group of marine mammals called pinnipeds (meaning fin-footed)–abound on the island's shores. With the relative lack of human disturbance, Anacapa is a safe haven for these mammals to warm up and rest after a long night of feeding.

The abundance of marine mammals, fish and invertebrates is a testament to the value of the healthy giant kelp forest and the protection from collection on most of the island's north shore. After many years of overxfishing of abalone, lobster and other fishes, these creatures are thriving once again in the offshore nutrient rich, cool, clear waters of Anacapa.

NATIVE PEOPLE HISTORY

Native people on Anacapa date over 5,000 years to the earliest people who came to the island. The discovery of the shell middens (native trash sites) on the island provides a window into this deep and intricate island heritage. Through these archeological sites, we can learn about the native Chumash people—a living culture today—their amazing history visiting the island, what they ate, clothes they wore and tools they used.

Archeologists' study of these sites allows them to weave together a part of the complex story of these skillful seafarers who thrived in their isolated paradise. Though no long-term settlements have been found on Anacapa, probably due to the lack of fresh water, the Chumash did use East Anacapa as a stopover when traveling between the islands and the mainland.

Its close proximity to modern day Port Hueneme—from the Chumash word *Wynema* meaning "half-way" or "resting place"—made for easier accessibility with a distance of only eleven miles from the mainland

"We have an opportunity to save this unique place and the awe inspiring creatures and plants that exist here and nowhere else from being lost forever. We can either act now to help restore this little island, or we can allow the damage we have done in the past to continue destroying what has taken nature many thousands of years to create. We have decided to act."

—Kevin Thompson, Operations Manager, Channel Islands Restoration

Arch Rock.

Top left and right: California sea lions bask in the sun on the craggy shores of Anacapa Island.
Bottom: Arch Rock below the lighthouse.

CATHEDRAL COVE

Giant coreopsis above Cathedral Cove.

Top: **Male California brown pelican in breeding plumage.**
Bottom left: **Pigeon guillemot.**
Bottom right: **Side-blotched lizard.**

COREOPSIS

Blooming in spring, the stunning giant coreopsis—a bizarre-looking member of the sunflower family—dazzles the eye as its brown, lifeless stalks erupt into bright yellow blossoms in late winter and early spring.

FRENCHY'S COVE

Left and above: Tide pools on West Anacapa Island.

Middle: California sea hare.

Bottom: Striped shore crabs.

Left: Western gull nests are frequently seen adjacent to the trails on East Anacapa.
Opposite page left: Western gull nesting at Inspiration Point.
Opposite page right and below: West Anacapa, with the exception of Frenchy's Cove and the tide pool area, is restricted to public access to protect the West Coast's primary nesting site of once endangered California brown pelicans.

Left: **Impressive displays of wildflowers cover East Anacapa Island following winter rains.**
Top: **Northern island tree mallow.**
Bottom: **Giant coreopsis.**

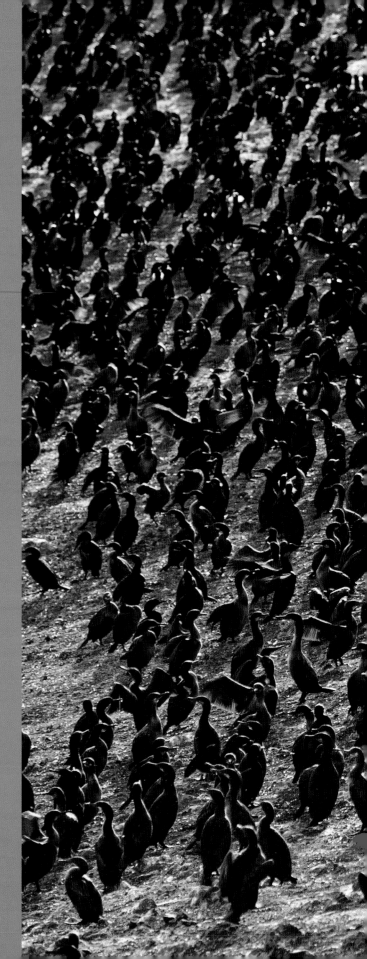

Above: **Say's Phoebe.**
Right: **Cormorants spread their wings in the warmth of the early morning sun near Arch Rock.**

Over 10,000 western gulls gather for nesting on Anacapa Island during the spring and summer months.

Top: **Naturalist led guided tours of the island include a walk up to the historic lighthouse.**
Bottom left: **School groups volunteer with many projects on Anacapa, including the ongoing vegetation restoration.**
Bottom right: **Live-forever.**
Opposite page: **Evening light settles on Anacapa Island.**

SANTA CRUZ ISLAND
the crown jewel

The largest body of land off the coast of California, Santa Cruz Island encompasses 96 square miles with 77 miles of pristine coastline. Near to millions of people yet so different from the mainland, Santa Cruz offers a peek into a way of life foreign to most people in Southern California. As in the 1800s, silence is undisturbed by electronic beeps and only the sound of waves lapping at the shore and the calls of soaring birds overhead are heard.

A mini-California geographically, the island has two rugged transverse mountain ranges with the highest peak rising over 2,400 feet above the ocean. Island highlights include a native Bishop pine forest, a large central valley and geologic fault system, deep canyons and ravines with year-round fresh springs and streams, crystal-clear tide pools and hundreds of sea caves including one of the world's largest and deepest sea caves, Painted Cave.

This amazing place hosts 60 of the 145 unique species found in Channel Islands National Park. Some, like the Santa Cruz Island scrub jay and the Santa Cruz Island silver lotus, are found here and nowhere else on earth.

Isolation has played an important role in the development of these rare animals and plants, but has also made them more vulnerable to human activities and the threat of extinction. Human endeavors introduced exotic plants that otherwise would not have existed here. Such invasive species can have a detrimental impact on the landscape and habitats.

The overgrazing of non-native animals and introduced non-native plants led to major destruction of the island's unique plant communities. European grasses and other exotic plants outcompeted the endemic species and soon took over large expanses of land causing extinction to some plants and near extinction to others. Feral pigs also caused major devastation to important archeological sites including damage to village and midden sites occupied by the Chumash native people for at least 9,000 years.

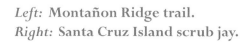

Left: **Montañon Ridge trail.**
Right: **Santa Cruz Island scrub jay.**

Chumash Natives

Before ranching began in the 1800s, native Chumash people populated the island with an intricate village system. At one time, scientists estimate that the island was home to over 2,000 Chumash who lived off the land and sea, successfully creating a sustainable island home.

For over 9,000 years, Chumash islanders ate shellfish varieties that were plentiful on the rocky shores and cliff sides including abalone, California mussels and clams. After the discovery of a hard glass-like sedimentary rock called chert, these creative people made tools to turn the plentiful olivella shells into bead money. The discovery of chert and creation of bead money aided the island people in trading for items they lacked on their remote islands.

These able seafarers also designed an advanced plank canoe, or *tomol* that allowed them to ply the deep surrounding waters for large fish such as tuna, halibut and California sheephead. This new ability to line and hook fish, as well as net fish, expanded their food and trade options too. They also made spears to aid in the collection of fish, seals and sea lions to use for food and clothing.

Explore the island today and you will find myriad shell middens that help tell the amazing story of these people and their time on the island, what food they ate and the tools they used. These historically significant sites provide a window into their deep and rich history on the island. Park staff and The Nature Conservancy work together so these special places will be protected into the future. Modern Chumash are working to preserve their past with present day traditions including an annual tomol crossing to Santa Cruz Island.

Below: **Cavern Point.**
Opposite page left: **Cavern Point.**   *Opposite page right:* **Cliffs above Scorpion Anchorage.**

RANCHING ERA

Ranching began in the early 1800s, but in 1880 when Justinian Caire controlled the island in its entirety, a ranching empire was born. The sheer size of the island made it difficult to run a successful operation. Steep ravines and large canyons made it a challenge to reach the central valley where the main ranch was located. The island's remoteness was also a key factor in the persistence it took to make a ranching operation successful.

To improve efficiency of operating on such a large and rugged land, Caire created nine "out ranches" with each being charged with specific responsibilities in support of the main ranching facilities in the island's central valley.

To preserve the rich ranching history of nearly 150 years, the National Park Service has restored two ranching bunkhouses on the island, one at Scorpion Anchorage and the other at Smugglers Cove. These two-story buildings were built in the 1880s from island-made adobe brick limestone quarried on the island. Wood that floated ashore from shipwrecks was often used as well in these early buildings.

Above and right: Scorpion Canyon Loop Trail.

Left: A cool resting stop on the way to Smugglers Cove is this grove of Monterey cypress, known as Delphine's Grove.

Above: Remnant of past ranching era along Scorpion Canyon Loop Trail.

RESTORING AND PRESERVING FOR THE FUTURE

Today, protection and preservation of island resources are divided between The Nature Conservancy, which owns and manages the western 76% of the island, and the National Park Service, which owns and operates the eastern 24%. Their combined efforts help to restore balance to the ecosystem, save unique species, including the Santa Cruz Island fox, from the brink of extinction and protect more than 3,000 internationally significant archeological sites.

From the mainland coast, the island looms in the distance, a large remote expanse sitting on the horizon. Upon closer inspection, the craggy cliffs sweep down to rocky beaches where volcanic rock meets the sparkling blue waters of the Pacific Ocean. Giant kelp forests, that under optimal conditions can grow two feet a day along the shoreline, provide a home, nursery, and feeding ground for about 800 species of fish, marine mammals and invertebrates.

Opposite page top left: **Mating butterflies.**
Opposite page top middle: **Santa Cruz Island ironwood.**
Opposite page top right: **Santa Cruz Island fox.**
Opposite page bottom left: **Santa Cruz Island scrub jay.**
Opposite page bottom right: **Restored wetland at Prisoners Harbor.**
Bottom left: **White-crowned sparrow.**
Bottom right: **Mallards.**

RESTORING BALANCE

In modern times, non-native feral piglets provided a year-round food source for golden eagles, allowing these previously infrequent island visitors an opportunity to expand their range and establish resident island populations. They then began to prey on island foxes leading to the near extinction of the endemic population. In addition DDT, a pesticide used after WWII, had a major effect on large fish-eating birds like the bald eagle and California brown pelican. Their eggshells did not harden properly because DDT led to a reduction in their calcium levels causing these birds to die off from population depletion because of an aging flock.

To restore balance, the golden eagles were captured and relocated to northeast California while the island foxes were put in a captive breeding program. Bald eagles that had previously thrived on the island were then reestablished to their historic habitat.

These recovery efforts are paying off. Island foxes are again thriving on Santa Cruz, Santa Rosa and San Miguel islands (all having been affected by golden eagle predation), and the bald eagle population has soared with multiple chicks being fledged over the past several years.

Bird habitat has also undergone major restoration through the cooperative works of the National Park Service, The Nature Conservancy and many other agencies. Where once a natural wetland provided good bird habitat near Prisoners Harbor, there is a newly reestablished wetland to restore one removed during the ranching era. This wetland is again thriving providing natural habitat for local and migrating birds.

Opposite page: Cavern Point Loop Trail above Scorpion Ranch.
Top left: Peregrine falcon. *Top right:* Cavern Point Loop Trail.
Bottom left: Anna's hummingbird. *Bottom middle:* Island tarweed. *Bottom right:* Dark-eyed junco.

Volcanic rock outcroppings like Scorpion Rock just offshore of Scorpion Landing was a historically significant nesting site. A major restoration project has returned these rocky outposts back to nesting seabirds—including the rare and threatened Cassin's auklet that spends its life at sea only coming ashore to nest once a year. The reestablishment of native habitat was possible through the joint efforts of several agencies with the help of historic journals and photographs depicting the types of flora that once existed.

Today's visitors can partake in the natural beauty of this wild landscape, once again see island foxes foraging in the wild, watch bald eagles soaring overhead, and enjoy water sports like kayaking, snorkeling or diving in the pristine waters offshore.

"I have seen dramatic changes on Santa Cruz Island in the past decade. The native and endemic plant communities are teeming, where once there were few. It's rewarding to experience these changes to the once barren landscape."

—Lee Fleischer, frequent island visitor

Opposite page: Scorpion Canyon Loop Trail.
Above left: Trail marker. *Above right:* Santa Cruz Island silver lotus.
Below: View from Montañon Ridge.

MONTAÑON RIDGE

An island scrub oak frames Anacapa Island. On the horizon at left are the Santa Monica Mountains.

Opposite page: **Profile Rock.**
Top left: **Swallow nests.** *Top right:* **Painted Cave.**
Bottom left: **Greene's live-forever.**
Bottom right: **Greene's live-forever and island red buckwheat near the entrance to Painted Cave.**

Kayaking, snorkeling, and boating are popular recreational activities at Scorpion Anchorage.

Kayakers explore sea caves and a blowhole near Potato Harbor.

Opposite page left: Pelican Bay with Tinkers Cove in the foreground.

Opposite page right: Canyon sunflowers along the trail between Prisoners Harbor and Pelican Bay.

Above left: Island monkey flower. *Above middle:* Woodmint, also known as hedge nettle. *Above right:* Humboldt lily.

Below: Prisoners Harbor.

SMUGGLERS COVE

SANTA ROSA ISLAND
old california

As you near Santa Rosa Island, Skunk Point comes into view; this luminous sand spit juts out into the Santa Barbara Channel and is one of the island's most striking features. The tiny snowy plover ground nests on the sandy shores and the giant kelp forests and rare eelgrass beds provide a nearshore nursery for a variety of fish and invertebrates.

Often referred to as "Cowboy Island" from its cattle ranching past, Santa Rosa provides a glimpse into what Southern California was like when island ranching began around 1840. Visitors making the long journey to Santa Rosa are rewarded with expansive white sand beaches, a beautifully sculpted windswept landscape, rolling forested hills, magnificent canyons, and the rare Torrey pine found in only two places in the world, Santa Rosa Island and San Diego County.

Left: **Indian paintbrush, California poppy, silver bush lupine, seaside daisy, and wild heliotrope create a kaleidoscope of color near Carrington Point.**
Top: **Anna's hummingbird.** *Bottom:* **An ochre sea star clings to a colony of sandcastle worms, sometimes called honeycomb worms, which are known for their reef building.**

A Feast for the Senses

At 83 square miles, Santa Rosa is the second largest of the eight Channel Islands and, the largest island fully owned by the National Park Service. The rare Torrey pine is a remnant from the Ice Age. The tide pools are pristine and teeming with life, the languidly rolling hills are dappled with unique island oak and Santa Rosa Island manzanita, vast coastal marine terraces provide exquisite views, and the largest coastal lagoon of all the islands makes it a great place to explore.

Mother Nature has been at work adding touches of color to the landscape with the scouring rush in the fresh water canyons, brightly hued endemic monkey flower, red variety island buckwheat and the giant coreopsis. The island also offers a diverse array of plant communities including grasslands, woodlands and Bishop pine groves.

"The rare Torrey Pine forest has a unique character, scent and sound. An island growing within an island, framing views of a white sand beach and diverse ocean habitat."
–Kathy deWet-Oleson, long-time Channel Islands visitor

A Step Back in Time

Visiting Santa Rosa, evidence of the long ranching history is one of the first things you notice. It is like taking a step back into old California with many historic ranch facilities, including old wooden fenced corrals, a bunkhouse, main house, red barns and a former schoolhouse.

The long ranching era began with sheep ranching starting in 1840. In 1902, the Vail and Vickers Company began cattle ranching on Santa Rosa. This is how the island got its moniker "Cowboy Island" from the vaqueros who rode on horseback, managing the herds. In 1909 non-native Roosevelt elk were introduced, followed by Kaibab mule deer in 1929.

Above: **A broken-down fence near the mouth of Lobo Canyon stands as a reminder of more than 150 years of ranching history on the island.**
Right top: **Island red buckwheat.** *Right bottom:* **Indian paintbrush.**
Opposite page top: **Historic main ranch.**
Opposite page bottom: **Lichen covered rocks dot the rolling hills of the island's interior.**

ANCIENT CULTURAL HISTORY

Santa Rosa has been home to native people as far back as about 13,000 years ago. Archeologists have found and dated the earliest known remains of humans in the western hemisphere at Arlington Springs. What scientists do not yet know is if the remains are from a Chumash ancestor who lived and thrived on the island for thousands of years or are indicative of another native or exploratory group. Still, the finding is significant and one of the reasons this island holds a unique status in understanding early human settlement in America.

The native Chumash named the island *Wimal*–meaning "redwood." There are no redwood trees on the island, but the Chumash plank canoe *tomol* builders preferred redwood to other types of trees due to its water absorption properties making for a tighter seam. Not in a rush to build their boats, they would wait for redwood to come ashore as it made its way from Northern California to the Santa Barbara Channel on the tides and currents and wind generated waves.

Santa Rosa Island has many historically significant midden sites that help us learn the rich and long history of the population of native Chumash who lived and thrived here for thousands of years. These archeological sites help us understand the life they led on their island home, the food they ate and the tools they used.

Above: **Cherry Canyon Trail.**
Right: **White sand beach at Water Canyon.**

NATURAL HISTORY
Native and Endemic Flora and Fauna

Archeologists discovered on Santa Rosa the most complete skeletal remains of a pygmy or Channel Islands mammoth; this relative to the Columbian mammoth made its way across the Santa Barbara Channel to the islands to munch on terrestrial plants and trees.

Over thousands of years, the mammoths shrunk from about fourteen feet at the shoulder to about four feet. Often referred to as the island effect, dwarfism was necessary for the animals to survive in a much smaller environment with limited food sources and less available water. Today, some scientists believe that the earliest humans on the island may have arrived when the smaller mammoths were still present. The mammoths were able to swim to the islands as the sea levels were lower and the shorelines extended further out.

As the pygmy mammoth became a smaller version of its larger cousin, so has isolation created a different type of Torrey pine distinct from its relative in San Diego. Many botanists believe that the pine is different enough from the mainland tree—located 175 miles away—that it should be considered a separate subspecies and be referred to as the Santa Rosa Island Torrey pine.

The island variety grows shorter, broader and bushier than its mainland cousin and its bark is thicker and scalier. The cones are rounder but like the San Diego variety it has needles in clusters of five. However, the island Torrey pine has vibrant blue-gray needles, while those on the mainland are grayish.

This rare pine has a limited range and is found only on two sandstone bluffs on the island's northeast corner. Its limited existence may qualify the island variety as not only the rarest native pine in the United States, but quite possibly the rarest pine in the world. No matter its designation, hiking through the pines is an amazing experience; the forest houses many varieties of plants scattered under its canopy, and beautifully grizzled old island manzanita trees are a treat for the eyes. Hikers get glimpses through the trees of the coastline and sparkling cerulean sea below.

With ranching came exotic or introduced plants that quickly overcame flora unique to the island. Native plants developed in isolation are vulnerable to competition from the hardier new species and become outcompeted. In addition, when plants develop in isolation, they waste no energy on building defenses like thorns or spines as protection against being eaten by non-native animals.

Opposite page: **Santa Rosa Island fox.**
Above left: **Golden yarrow in a field of wild hyacinth.** *Above right:* **Munchkin dudleya – a flower endemic to East Point.**

RESTORING AND PROTECTING

When non-native livestock are brought into an isolated environment, they feed and trample upon native plants without much difficulty and cause devastation to the natural landscape.

Today, of the 500 plant species found on Santa Rosa Island, 36 are endemic to the Channel Islands and found nowhere else. Six of these species occur only on Santa Rosa Island, including the munchkin dudleya, and some are considered threatened or endangered. Without protection provided by the National Park Service, these plants might be lost forever.

Sheep had previously been removed during the beginning of the Vail and Vickers era, but by then a lot of damage had already been done to the island plant communities. At one point, there were over 100,000 sheep grazing on Santa Rosa. A number well over the carrying capacity of the island, there was simply not enough food to maintain that many sheep. Even today, over 100 years later we still see evidence of excessive erosion from that period.

Cattle were removed from the island in 1998 and the non-native deer and elk have been removed as well. The Park Service continues to control the spread of the non-native weeds like fennel, thistle and mustard in an effort to help the native vegetation recoup.

Today there is increasing hope native vegetation will recover through these restorative efforts. We are now seeing these unique species starting to repopulate the entire island landscape, where once many of the native plants were only found on steep cliff faces not accessible to livestock.

National Park staff is monitoring the vast island, recording the native, endemic plants and trees. A fog study is ongoing to help botanists understand the role the moist marine air plays in the growth of the local flora. Currently, a large woodland of island oak–the rarest of all oaks–is being restored through the regeneration of soil and restoration of the understory of native plant species. An island nursery established for growing native flora from seeds collected on the island is giving a much needed boost to nature in the reestablishment of native plants.

As on Santa Cruz and San Miguel islands, the island fox population also crashed on Santa Rosa. The predation by golden eagles, previously not known to nest and live on the island, took the fox population down by 90% during the 1990s. The Santa Rosa Island foxes were put in a captive breeding program on the island and are now all living in the wild and the population is on the upswing. This improvement in the fox population allows visitors a greater chance to catch a glimpse of the diminutive mammals foraging around the island.

With the reintroduction of bald eagles on the island, visitors are reporting sightings of adult and juvenile bald eagles. Peregrine falcon and osprey populations that were also impacted by the effects of DDT are growing as well. It is now more commonplace to see osprey with a fish in its talons or view peregrine falcons soaring overhead.

Work is underway to preserve and restore the historic ranch buildings as well so that visitors to Santa Rosa can gain a sense of connection with old California, and imagine what it might have been like to live and ranch on this remote island.

With the end of the elk and deer hunt, the island is now fully open for park visitors to hike the rolling hills and the wind sculpted canyons, beach comb the crystal sand shoreline and dream of a time when cowboys were indeed kings on this windswept landscape.

Left: **Black Rock.** *Above:* **Pigeon guillemot.**

Left: **California sea lions.**
Top: **Natural arch.**
Bottom: **Indian pink.**

JOHNSONS LEE

Top: Windswept island scrub oak at South Point.
This species is endemic to the Channel Islands.
Bottom: Northern elephant seals.
Right: Tide pool channel.

CHINA CAMP BEACH

Lobo Canyon

"Seemingly endless winds have gracefully sculpted the sandstone walls overhead; yet even on the windiest days, I find hiking the floor of Lobo Canyon provides refuge. It's a magical place."

–Kathy deWet-Oleson, long-time Channel Islands visitor

Harbor seal pup.

SKUNK POINT

SUNRISE–CARRINGTON POINT

SAN MIGUEL ISLAND
island in the mist

Harsh winds and misty sea air batter the shores of the westernmost of the Channel Islands, San Miguel. This extreme weather has shaped a profoundly beautiful island landscape. The all too common fog often clears by midday and the landscape finally emerges and begins to take shape for a brilliant but short afternoon. Mountainous sand dunes sparkle in the midday sun while the aquamarine sea laps on the sandy beaches below Nidever Canyon.

The island area, including Prince Island which lies at the entrance of Cuyler Harbor, measures 14 square miles, or about 9,400 acres. As you approach, the island appears to be a plateau of about 500 feet elevation but as you climb up Nidever Canyon to reach that plateau, two 800-foot rounded hills emerge from the wild, windswept landscape.

Today, lush native vegetation covers the island following a century's worth of sheep ranching and overgrazing. In fact, it had been so overgrazed that scientists in 1875 surveying the island described it as "a barren lump of sand."

The appearance of the caliche forest (sand castings of ancient vegetation) is in stark contrast to the verdant vegetation seen in most areas of the island today. Scientists have found fossilized bones of the Pleistocene pygmy mammoths on this island. It is also the site of one of the oldest human archeological sites at 11,600 years before present time.

Famed Spanish explorer Juan Rodriguez Cabrillo was the first European to visit the island in 1542. Centuries following his death—it was believed he died from an injury while on the island—a memorial in his honor was built there. Speculation continues today as to where he died and where he is buried.

Northern elephant seals and Western gulls, Cardwell Point.

RANCHING ERA

Though never privately owned, ranching began on San Miguel Island in the 1840s by squatters. However, ranching was unsuccessful until George Nidever and his sons leased the island from the U.S. government and began sheep ranching on the island in 1850. By 1862, ranch livestock included 6,000 sheep, 200 cattle, 100 hogs and 32 horses.

The livestock was well over the natural carrying capacity for the island–there was simply not enough food to feed that many sheep. When the drought of 1863-1864 hit, 5,000 of the sheep died and the others devoured everything in sight in search of life sustaining moisture.

The earliest island ranch house was located in Nidever Canyon. Its remains were swallowed by drifting sand. 1n 1906, rancher William Waters constructed the island's largest ranch house. He salvaged materials from shipwrecks around the island to build it–mostly out of lumber from the schooner *J.M. Coleman* that went aground inside Point Bennett in 1905. The structure measured 125 feet long and 16 feet wide with double-walls to withstand the strong winds. A blacksmith shop/harness room, tool shed, well, cistern, and root cellar were also constructed.

Herbert Lester managed the ranch from 1929-1942 bringing his new socialite bride with him to the island. They had two daughters and enjoyed the isolated island life. As Lester put it, the remote living was an escape "from the shallowness of civilization and its incessant and inconsequential demands."

San Miguel soon came to be known as Lester's Island; as did William Waters' before him, Lester called himself King of San Miguel. He wore a makeshift insignia to designate his rank and the family's mailbag read "Kingdom of San Miguel." Stories abound from the Lester era due to extensive coverage in the press, a *Life* magazine article published in 1940, and several books written about his time on the island.

Above left: Black-bellied plovers.   *Above right:* Pelagic cormorant.
Below: An area above Cuyler Harbor, referred to as the Wind Tunnel, is sandblasted
bare by the harsh winds for which San Miguel Island is well known.

REMARKABLE NATIVE PLANT RECOVERY

With so many years of overgrazing by sheep on the island, introduced plants soon overtook the natives. There are 18 plant species on San Miguel Island unique to the Channel Islands. Today four of these have been lost and another four species are listed as endangered or threatened. Without protection, these special plants could become extinct and lost forever.

To ensure the survival of these unique species and encourage the recovery of the island's native vegetation, National Park staff has worked towards the removal of non-native species. To this end, by 1966 sheep were removed from the island and burros by 1977.

In addition to exotic animal removal, the National Park Service has been controlling the spread of non-native weeds like fennel, fireweed, thistle and mustard helping to further the reestablishment of the native island flora.

Just by removing non-native plants and animals, the island has experienced a major native plant recovery. Today, most of the island is covered with native and endemic vegetation.

Above: **Lichen covered bluffs above Glass Float Beach.**
Right: **Northern elephant seals at Cardwell Point.**

Native Animals and Marine Mammals Recovery

The island fox population on San Miguel suffered from golden eagle predation as it did on Santa Cruz and Santa Rosa islands. After the successful removal of the golden eagles, removal of feral pigs and the reintroduction of bald eagles on neighboring islands, San Miguel's foxes have made a huge recovery as well.

The pre-crash population of the island's foxes was about 450 in 1990. In 1998, only 15 could be located in the wild. The fox populations are recovering and these diminutive mammals are thriving on the island once again.

After ending the many years of hunting seals and sea lions for their pelts and oil, the island's marine mammal populations made an amazing comeback. Increased populations of California sea lions, Northern fur seals, Northern elephant seals, and harbor seals breed, pup, and haul out on the island's 27 miles of isolated coastline. Smaller populations of Steller sea lions and Guadalupe fur seals are occasional visitors to the island.

Hikers who make the all-day, ranger-guided trek to Point Bennett--16 miles round-trip--will never forget seeing one of the world's most spectacular wildlife displays. Visitors can see four different populations of seals and sea lions by the thousands during their breeding times on Harris Point and Point Bennett beaches.

Opposite page: **California sea lions and Northern elephant seals mingle on a beach in Cuyler Harbor.**
Top: **Horned lark.**
Bottom: **San Miguel Island fox.**

REBUILD IT AND THEY WILL COME

San Miguel Island and its offshore islets, Prince Island and Castle Rock, support regionally important and diverse seabird colonies, including one-third of the breeding seabirds in the Channel Islands.

The National Park Service has worked to reestablish seabird nesting habitats at San Miguel Island and its offshore islets. Seabirds targeted for this recovery project include the ashy storm petrel, Cassin's auklet and Scripps's murrelet, western gull, Brandt's cormorant, common murre and pigeon guillemot.

In July 2011, California common murre chicks (murres are abundant off the central and north coast of California) had hatched for the first time since 1912 on the Channel Islands. This species had historically nested on Prince Island, but disappeared nearly a century ago due to human disturbance and egg harvesting.

With the addition of this murre colony, Prince Island now hosts 13 species of nesting seabirds, making it one of the most important and biologically diverse nesting habitats on the west coast of North America. This important seabird habitat sits within Channel Islands National Park, the Channel Islands National Marine Sanctuary and the Harris Point marine protected area.

A visit to Cuyler Harbor at San Miguel offers an opportunity to see these avian species flying to and from their native nesting sites.

Above: **Simonton Cove.**
Right: **Harris Point.**

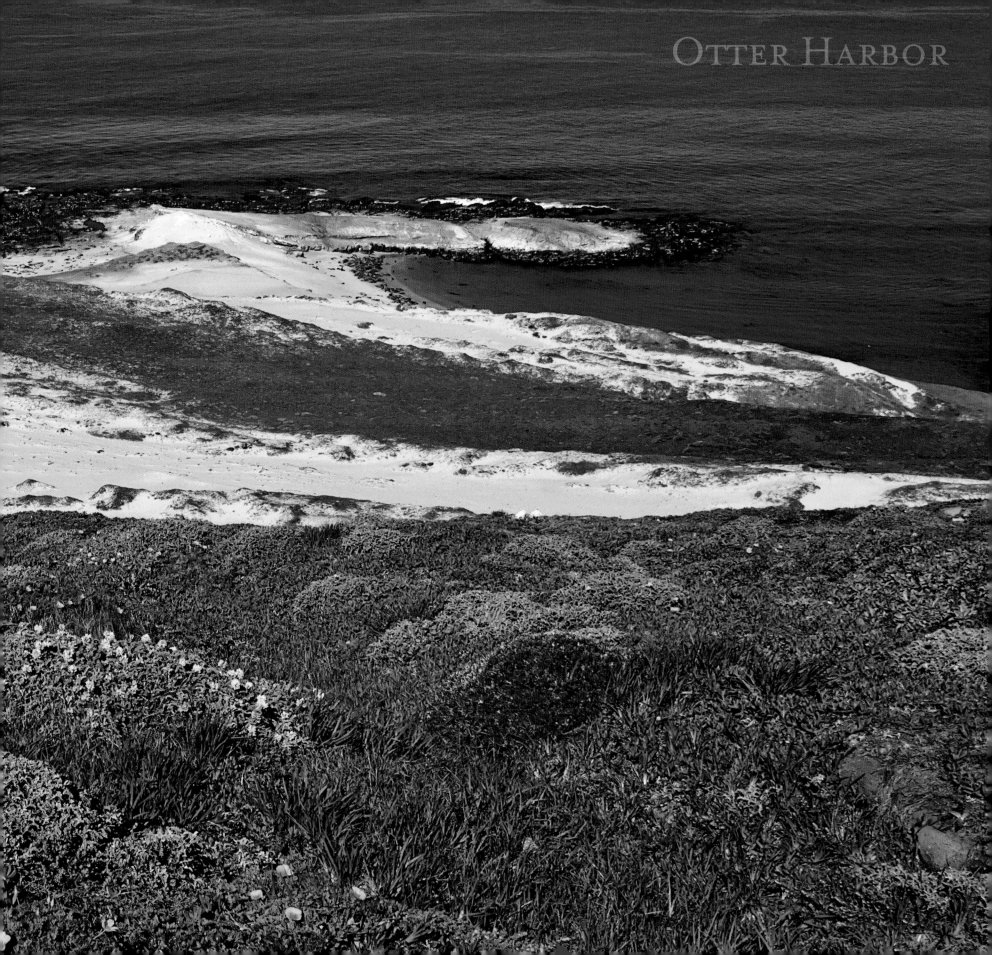

> *"Returning to San Miguel Island each year to see the robust breeding colonies of raucous California sea lions, or the Northern elephant seals, has refreshed my hopes and dreams that, with or without us, the Channel Islands will endure as an inspirational refuge."*
>
> —Brent S. Stewart, Ph.D., J.D., Hubbs-SeaWorld Research Institute

Every year, thousands of pinnipeds (seals and sea lions) breed, pup, and haul out on the island's 27 miles of isolated coastline.
Top: Crook Point. *Bottom:* California sea lions. *Right:* Point Bennett.

NORTHERN
ELEPHANT SEALS

Left: Northern elephant seals.

Top: Cardwell Point with Santa Rosa in the background.

Bottom: Curious female at Point Bennett.

Left: Cabrillo's Monument overlooking Cuyler Harbor. Prince Island, a forty-acre island located within Cuyler Harbor, has the densest seabird colony in Southern California, with thirteen different breeding species.
Above: A springtime display of giant coreopsis.

Cuyler Harbor from Lester Trail.

Simonton Cove has one of the oldest human archeological sites dated 11,600 years before present time.

Above left to right: Northern elephant seals, Northern fur seals, Northern elephant seals and California sea lions, Northern elephant seal bull and calf.
Below: Point Bennett.

SANTA BARBARA ISLAND
crossroads

Situated 38 miles offshore of mainland California lies the tiniest and southernmost of the five islands that make up Channel Islands National Park. As you near the island, it seems to emerge from the ocean as a giant twin-peaked mesa with steep cliffs and sloping marine terraces. Two rounded hills–Signal Peak and North Peak–come into view as do narrow rocky beaches that are usually underwater at high tide.

On a clear day, those who hike to Signal Peak (elevation 635 feet) get a stunning 360-degree view. From this locale, it is possible to see six of the other Channel Islands–San Clemente, Santa Catalina, San Nicolas, Anacapa, Santa Cruz and Santa Rosa. San Miguel Island is not visible from this vantage point as it is hidden from view by Santa Rosa Island. California sea lions, harbor seals and Northern elephant seals can often be seen hauled out on beaches and outlying rocks. In this remote wilderness, one hears the sound of nature, the barking of sea lions, the calling of soaring birds and the lapping of the Pacific on the island's craggy shoreline.

Santa Barbara Island had no permanent Native American settlements, but native Chumash people did travel to this isle to trade with natives from Santa Catalina Island, the Tongva natives. No fresh water is available, so they had to bring water in their woven watertight containers. Midden sites exist on Santa Barbara as on the other islands and help tell the rich history of these early people who still reside on the California mainland today.

Left: **Western gull protecting its territory near Elephant Seal Cove.**
Right: **Nesting California brown pelicans.**

RANCHING HISTORY

Santa Barbara Island was never privately owned and in 1905, the U.S. government reserved the island for a lighthouse, but one was never built. A few years later, the Hyder family obtained a lease to ranch on the island. With no predators to harm livestock—the largest land mammal being only the endemic deer mouse—and being surrounded by ocean meant no need for fencing and no evidence of disease, the family set to work.

The long distance from the mainland proved to be an ongoing challenge for the import of fresh water, livestock and supplies. The trip to the mainland, commonly accompanied by rough seas and frequent gale storm winds that pushed the ocean into 15-foot waves, made it a hard fought battle to ranch the land and make a living.

The Hyders spent nine challenging years trying to establish a diverse ranch that would allow them to be self-sufficient and profitable. They raised a variety of crops and imported many different animals including sheep, horses, mules, rabbits, ducks, geese, turkeys and chickens. Traders and other visitors also brought cats to the island, most likely in the last century.

Opposite page left: **Island tarweed and Santa Barbara Island buckwheat on the slopes of North Peak, overlooking Webster Point.**
Opposite page right: **Santa Barbara Island buckwheat, endemic to Santa Barbara Island, is recovering along the slopes of North Peak.**
Below: **Goldfields along the Arch Point Loop Trail.**

RETURN OF NATIVE PLANTS AND ANIMALS

The island's isolation, freedom from most predators and human disturbance, and the abundance of food in the cold ocean waters makes it an ideal place for seabirds to breed and rear their young. Santa Barbara Island is one of the largest breeding locales for western gulls in the U.S.

As on Anacapa Island, thousands of western gulls nest every year on the island, some right along the trailside during the nesting season from May through July. When you see western gulls on the mainland, there is a very good chance that they hatched right here just offshore on one of these two islands.

California brown pelicans typically nest and raise their young on the island from January through October. If disturbed, the pelicans will abandon their nests, leaving the eggs and chicks defenseless against predators such as gulls and ravens; a serious disturbance can cause an entire colony to be abandoned. Santa Barbara Island's isolation is critical for the successful nesting of these birds.

The island also provides a home to significant colonies of both surface and crevice-nesting seabirds existing on the one square mile landmass and its even smaller offshore islets. These small isles host over 50% of the U.S. nesting population of the threatened Scripps's murrelet, representing about 20% of the global population of this rare seabird's breeding individuals.

However, due to ranching and other human activities, widespread destruction of the seabird colonies occurred in the past with bird populations heavily impacted by introduced predators. Similarly, native plant communities that supported the nesting Cassin's auklet needed much help to recover from the devastation of non-native shrubs and succulents and the ranching removal of plant cover in some areas. Invasive plants brought in during ranching and military activities over the past century caused much of the destruction.

The National Park Service continues to work toward the reestablishment of native plant communities and to restore shrub communities for nesting seabirds. These efforts are being rewarded with many avian species returning to their island nesting ground.

Opposite page: California sea lions at Landing Cove.
Above: California sea lions and Northern elephant seals at Elephant Seal Cove.

This multi-year effort included the planting of native flora like Santa Cruz Island buckwheat, silver lace and giant coreopsis, with the intention to mimic the natural habitat that once existed. Using journals from the 1800s and old photos of what had grown there, they established a plan to bring back the plant communities and entice the birds to return.

All 7,000 reestablished plants on the island were grown from seeds collected and propagated there in a shade house built for this purpose. Hundreds of volunteers worked with park staff to trudge materials uphill, grow and plant, and build an irrigation system using a solar-powered marine booster pump to draw water from a storage tank attached to a drip system.

Both the Scripps's murrelet and the Cassin's auklet are again nesting on this safe haven and are rebuilding their populations. The native plant communities have gone through a massive regeneration and the island is again alive with native and endemic plants.

Left top: **Santa Barbara Island live-forever (endemic).**
Left bottom: **Seaside cistanthe.**
Below: **Scripps's murrelet.**
Opposite page: **Nest of an island horned lark, a subspecies endemic to Santa Barbara Island.**

Left: Webster Point and North Peak from Signal Peak.

Top: Santa Barbara Island chicory.

Bottom: Santa Barbara Island cream cup.

--both are endemic to Santa Barbara Island.

Top: Trask's locoweed. *Bottom:* Silver lace.
--both are endemic to Santa Barbara Island.
Right: Shag Rock.

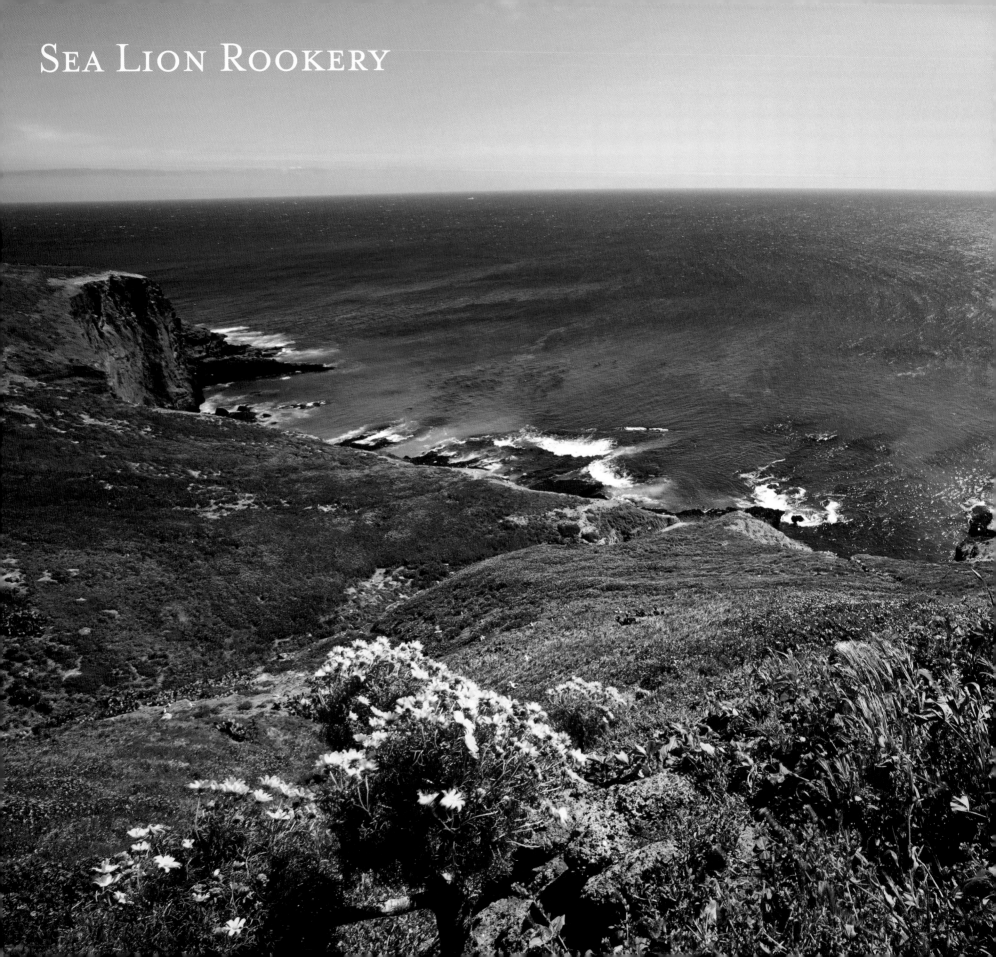

Left: Spectacular giant coreopsis dominates this view of the island's rocky shoreline.
Top: A floating classroom aboard a tall ship, anchored near the Sea Lion Rookery.
Bottom: Kayakers exploring the rugged coastline.

Left: Sutil Island.
Top: Prickly pear cactus.
Middle: Sutil Island from Signal Peak.
Bottom: Silver lotus.

Top: The trail to Webster Point leads through one of the largest western gull rookeries in the Channel Islands.

Bottom: Cormorants, California brown pelicans, and California sea lions can often be seen along the rocks and shores at Webster Point.

Right: Giant coreopsis on Signal Peak, with Webster Point in the background.

Webster Point.

THE SEA
worlds apart

Under the glimmering ocean lies a world of mystery that few people ever see. The crystal waters of the Channel Islands host the wonders of the sea and are a special place for visitors to enjoy a variety of water sports like boating, kayaking, fishing, snorkeling and scuba diving.

Park boundaries extend one nautical mile offshore providing a safe haven for many species near extinction, while protecting over 100 historically significant shipwrecks and native people's artifacts. The water extending six nautical miles offshore of the islands is the Channel Islands National Marine Sanctuary.

In this undersea world, there is a fertile combination of warm and cool currents resulting in a plethora of plant, animal, and algae species in the large nearshore giant kelp forests.

Populations of fish and invertebrates teem in the pristine waters and a diverse population of cetaceans, seals, sea lions and marine birds thrive in the secluded and relatively undisturbed waters. Threatened and protected animals living in and visiting these waters include blue, humpback and sei whales, Southern sea otters, California brown pelicans and California least terns.

More than 33 species of cetaceans (whales, dolphins and porpoises) use the park and sanctuary during at least part of the year. There are four species of seals and sea lions that live and breed here, over 60 species of birds feed in park and sanctuary waters, and more than 23 species of sharks occur here.

Left: **Octopus.** *(Photo © Richard Salas)*
Below: **Humpback whale tail.**

Common dolphin reflection.

CULTURAL HERITAGE

Prehistorically the islands were a special place to Native Americans known as Chumash who traveled to the islands in their sea worthy plank canoes called *tomols*, fishing the waters and traveling the sea for trade with other peoples. Today, a thriving Chumash community celebrates, as did their ancestors, their deep connection to the islands through annual tomol crossings to Santa Cruz Island; revitalization of their native language, dances and songs; and through sharing their history with local community members.

From the first Native Americans who plied the near and offshore waters of the park and sanctuary to modern times, artifacts, archeological sites and shipwrecks have been left behind, weaving a story of exploration and pioneering through the ages.

Discovery of these historically significant sites and relics gives us clues about how people lived, what they knew, and where they traveled. Over 150 historic ships and aircraft have been reported lost within park and sanctuary waters, yet only 25 of these have been discovered so far.

"These islands and waters are an ancestral and spiritual homeland for the first stewards of this special place, the Chumash people. It is also a global hotspot of biodiversity that needs protection. By working with the Chumash we can learn from their wisdom as they continue traditional practices drawn from their rich maritime heritage."

—Chris Mobley, Superintendent, Channel Islands National Marine Sanctuary

Above: **Chumash tomol crossing to Santa Cruz Island**

Photo © Robert V. Schwemmer, NOAA, Channel Islands National Marine Sanctuary

WHALES, DOLPHINS AND PORPOISES

One-third of the world's whale, dolphin and porpoise species are seen regularly in the park and sanctuary with some considered "residents." The sanctuary lies on the migratory pathway of the California gray whale and other large baleen and toothed whales. Gray whale cows and calves are observed in the nearshore kelp beds of the islands during their northward migration to Alaska. Gigantic blue whales—the largest animal to have ever existed on the planet—are sighted each year feeding in the nutrient rich sea.

Having rebounded from near extinction, four other species of marine mammals abound here as well: Northern elephant seal, California sea lion, Northern fur seal and harbor seal. The Steller sea lion and Guadalupe fur seal are occasional visitors to the area. Divers, snorkelers and boaters can catch sight of these agile mammals in the pristine waters offshore of the park islands.

One of the more awe-inspiring sights in the waters of the Channel Islands is that of a breaching humpback whale.

HUMPBACK WHALES

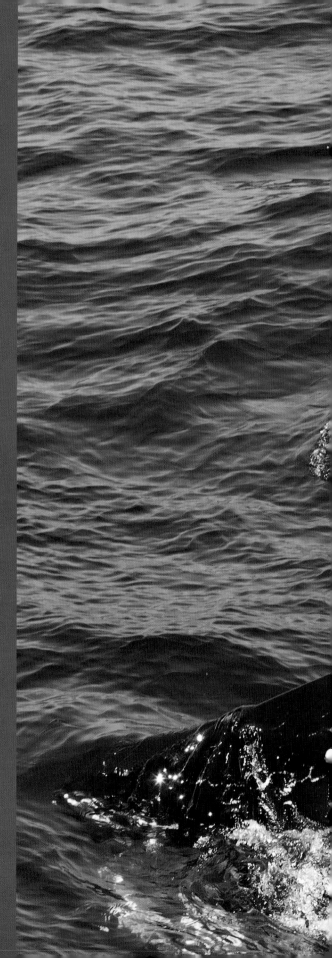

Top: Tail slap. *Bottom:* Friendly encounter.
Right: Lunge feeding.

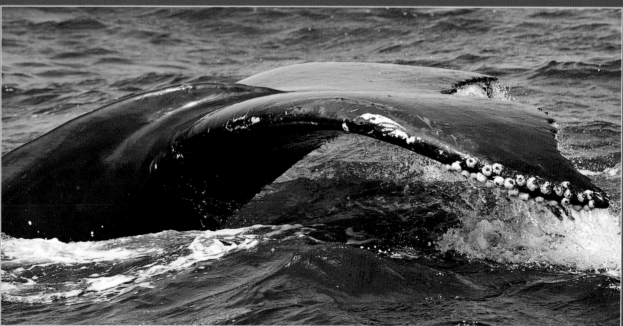

Humpback whales are among the most active and gregarious cetaceans in the waters of the Channel Islands.

Top: **Humpback whale pair.**
Bottom: **Blue whale cow and calf.**
Right: **Gray whale cow and calf.**

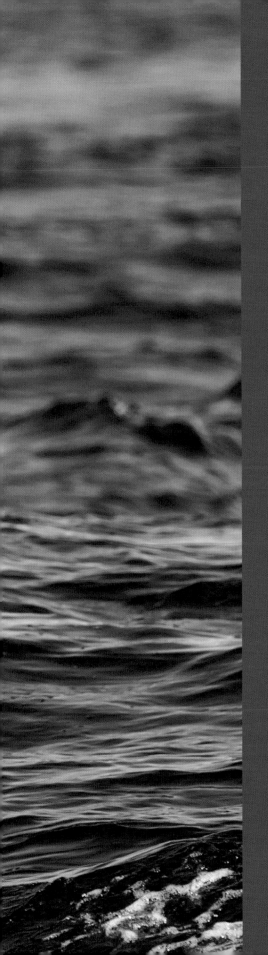

Left: **Bottle nose dolphin.**
Top: **Risso's dolphins.**
Bottom: **Common dolphins.**

Common dolphins at Arch Rock, Anacapa Island.

SEABIRDS

Over 60 species of marine birds use the Channel Islands for nesting and feeding habitat. Many winter here or migrate using the area as a stopover. Of the sixteen resident species of marine birds in the Southern California coastal region, thirteen breed in or near the northern Channel Islands. San Miguel Island supports the most numerous and diverse of these populations.

Santa Barbara Island has several nationally and internationally significant seabird nesting areas, including the largest nesting Scripps's murrelet colony and the only nesting site in the U.S. of black storm petrels. The California brown pelican maintains its only permanent rookery in California on Anacapa Island.

Top: **California brown pelicans.**
Above: **Pelagic cormorants.**
Opposite page left: **Scripps's murrelet.**
Opposite page right: **California brown pelican feeding frenzy.**

UNDER THE SEA

The mix of warm and cold water currents creates an amazing array of intertidal and subtidal life. Marine fauna species flourish in the transition zones that provide excellent habitat like rock shelves, boulder beaches, tide pools, rubble piles and sand flats. These habitats host a variety of creatures including acorn barnacles, periwinkles, limpets, chitons, sea stars, green anemones, shore crabs, brown, red and green algae, and California mussels.

The luxuriant forest-like growth of giant kelp are found along protected island shorelines and provide rich habitat for a variety of species like sponge, kelp crab, spiny lobster, octopus and squid, sea stars and sea urchins. Common kelp forest fish, including garibaldi, opal eye, kelp bass, California sheephead, sea perch and rockfish, abound in these waters. Other common sea creatures live in the sandy habitat including sea pansies, polychaetes, sand dollars, and several species of rays, sand dabs and turbots.

Top left: **California hydrocoral.** *Top right:* **Red sea urchin surrounded by purple urchins.**
Bottom left: **Giant keyhole limpet.** *Bottom right:* **Giant spined star.**
Opposite page: **Sunflower star.**

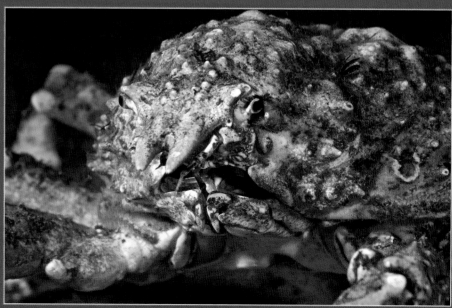

Opposite page top: Jack mackerel. *Opposite page bottom left:* Horn shark. *Opposite page bottom right:* Sheep crab (Spider crab).

Left top: Spanish shawl. *Left middle:* Male California garibaldi. *Left bottom:* Gopher rockfish.

Top: Lingcod. *Bottom:* Soupfin shark.

All photos © Richard Salas

California sea lion

(Photo © Richard Sala